The
Franklin
Roosevelts

by
Cass R. Sandak

CRESTWOOD HOUSE
New York

Maxwell Macmillan Canada
Toronto

Maxwell Macmillan International
New York Oxford Singapore Sydney

Library of Congress Cataloging-in-Publication Data
Sandak, Cass R.
    The Franklin Roosevelts / by Cass R. Sandak. — 1st ed.
        p. cm. — (First families)
    Includes bibliographical references and index.
    Summary: Describes the life and unprecedented four terms of the popular president, with an emphasis on his partnership with his wife, Eleanor.
    ISBN 0-89686-639-4
    1. Roosevelt, Franklin D. (Franklin Delano), 1882–1945—Juvenile literature. 2. Roosevelt, Eleanor, 1884–1962—Juvenile literature. 3. Presidents—United States—Biography—Juvenile literature. 4. Presidents—United States—Wives—Biography—Juvenile literature. [1. Roosevelt, Franklin D. (Franklin Delano), 1882–1945. 2. Roosevelt, Eleanor, 1884–1962. 3. Presidents. 4. First ladies.] I. Title. II. Series: Sandak, Cass R. First families.
E807.S25   1992
973.917'0922—dc20
[B]   91-30256
                                                                                              CIP
                                                                                              AC

Photo Credits
All photos courtesy of AP—Wide World Photos.

CRESTWOOD HOUSE

Macmillan Publishing Company
866 Third Avenue
New York, NY 10022

Maxwell Macmillan Canada, Inc.
1200 Eglinton Avenue East
Suite 200
Don Mills, Ontario M3C 3N1

Macmillan Publishing Company is part of the Maxwell Communication Group of Companies.

Produced by Flying Fish Studio

Printed in the United States of America

First edition

10 9 8 7 6 5 4 3 2 1

Contents

December 8, 1941. President Roosevelt appears before Congress, asking for an immediate declaration of war against Japan

"A Date Which Will Live in Infamy"

It was a wintry Sunday. The date was December 7, 1941. Many Americans were enjoying a lazy afternoon. Some were listening to the NBC Symphony broadcast with conductor Arturo Toscanini. But the calm was about to be shattered.

Suddenly radio broadcasts were interrupted. All America was told that the U.S. naval base at Pearl Harbor had been struck earlier that morning by Japanese bombers. No one was sure how many people had died during the surprise attack, but it was probably several thousand.

The news had come first to Washington. The president, Franklin Delano Roosevelt, was, like most Americans, enjoying the quiet Sunday. He was working on his stamp collection when aides interrupted him to tell of the terrible event.

The attack meant only one thing: The United States would have to go to war. Until that moment the war had been taking place in Europe. But now that Americans had been killed in U.S. territory, we would have to enter.

President Roosevelt signing the declaration of war against Germany

The next day the president called an emergency session of Congress. On that day, December 8, his son James helped the president make his way to the microphone. Roosevelt read a speech that began: "Yesterday, December 7, 1941—a date which will live in infamy—the United States of America was suddenly and deliberately attacked by naval and air forces of the Empire of Japan. . . . " Six minutes later the speech was over. Within half an hour Congress had declared war on Japan. For the United States and its people, World War II had begun.

Roosevelt's presidency—the longest ever—was forged in difficult times. When he became president in 1933 the United States was in its worst economic depression ever. No sooner had that situation begun to right itself than Adolf Hitler's armies began their march across Europe. And Japan threatened to conquer the Pacific. The times were hard for everyone, but especially for the gentleman from Hyde Park.

Young Franklin

Franklin Delano Roosevelt was born into a life of privilege. His mother, Sara Delano, had grown up on the Hudson close to her future husband's estate, Springwood, near Hyde Park. She was descended from a family that traced its roots in America back to the second shipload of colonists at Plymouth. More recently the family tree included many New England merchants and whalers.

Franklin Delano Roosevelt at age three riding on a donkey with his dog Budgy

Sara Delano and James Roosevelt were married in 1880. She was 26 and he was 52. Even though James was twice Sara's age, he was still a vigorous and active man. Two years later Franklin Delano Roosevelt was born in the Springwood house on January 30, 1882. Franklin was the only child the couple had.

Roosevelt's father was a businessman who lived off the income from his widespread investments. He also served on the boards of several large corporations. James Roosevelt had been born at the family estate on the Hudson. He took an active interest in running the estate and its farms. He was also an avid sportsman.

Eight-year-old Franklin Roosevelt playing with a bow and arrow

*Portrait of Franklin Roosevelt
as a teenager with his mother
and father*

The Springwood estate is in New York's lower Hudson Valley. Not far from the house was a well-equipped stable of champion racehorses. Despite more than 50 years' difference in their ages, father and son enjoyed a close relationship. Riding the trails on the estate was one of their favorite activities.

The banks of the Hudson were a few hundred yards below the house. Franklin learned to swim and to skate and to pilot a boat. It was an ideal place for a boy to grow up strong, active and free spirited.

The Roosevelts were part of the Hudson River aristocracy—old families of Dutch and English ancestry who had lived in the valley for more than 200 years. These families had inherited land and wealth and were joined by newcomers who had made their fortunes in the world of business—families such as the Vanderbilts.

Like other members of their social class, the Roosevelts had enough money to make life a pleasant round of parties and guests, sports and travel. This was the social world into which young Franklin was born. By blood or marriage, FDR could claim relationship to 11 former presidents: Washington, both Adamses, Madison, Van Buren, both Harrisons, Taylor, Grant, Theodore Roosevelt and his successor, Taft.

The Roosevelt family had a summer cottage on Campobello Island. The island is off the coast of Maine in Canadian waters. Every summer when Franklin was a boy, the family spent several weeks relaxing at this seaside resort.

Young Franklin was tutored at home. People of his class did not send their children to public schools. Nor did he have many young friends. The rich did not allow their children to mingle with the children of workers.

By the time he was a teenager, young Franklin had already sailed eight times to Europe with his parents. When he was 14 Franklin was sent to Groton, an exclusive private school in Massachusetts. He spent four years there and finished with reasonably strong grades.

When Franklin graduated from Groton, he enrolled at Harvard University in Cambridge, Massachusetts. In September 1900 he entered the class of 1904 as a freshman. There young Franklin joined the newspaper staff. He worked his way up through the *Harvard Crimson*'s ranks to become its president and editor in chief. It was as editor of the *Crimson* that he made his greatest impact at Harvard.

Franklin Roosevelt (front row, center) *when he was a member of the Groton football team*

Franklin majored in history and government. He could have finished Harvard in only three years. But he was so taken with his work on the newspaper that he stayed to complete his fourth, or senior, year.

Almost from the beginning, Sara was to be the dominant force in Franklin's life. James Roosevelt died of a heart ailment during Franklin's freshman year at Harvard. His father was 72 years old.

When Franklin graduated from Harvard it was expected that he would return to Hyde Park. There he would have a leisurely life as a wealthy estate owner and gentleman. At least that is what his recently widowed mother thought would happen. But she was wrong. Franklin had other plans, which included a career and marriage.

Eleanor Roosevelt as a young girl

Young Eleanor

Eleanor Roosevelt was born on October 11, 1884, in New York City. Her family had been prominent in the life of the city for several generations. She was a fifth cousin once removed of the man she came to marry, Franklin Delano Roosevelt. Eleanor's mother was Anna Rebecca Hall Roosevelt, an exceptionally beautiful woman. Eleanor's father was Elliott Roosevelt, the younger brother of Theodore Roosevelt. He was a gentle and sensitive man, but he was unsuccessful and an alcoholic.

Eleanor was only eight when her mother died of diphtheria. She and her younger brother, Hall, were sent to live with their maternal grandmother Hall. Grandmother Hall was a difficult woman, stern and distant.

Eleanor's mother had had a habit of calling the young girl "Granny," because of Eleanor's serious nature. Her mother had made her nervous—she had insisted on being present when Eleanor had lessons with her tutor. For this reason Eleanor started out as a poor student, even though she struck most people as a creative and intelligent child.

Eleanor always remembered the times spent with her father as the best part of her early life. But Elliott's fast living and hard drinking led to an early death. He died after a serious fall when he was drunk. Eleanor was two months short of her tenth birthday.

The knowledge that her mother had been a society beauty did not help Eleanor as she was growing up. Grandmother Hall and other relatives frequently reminded Eleanor that she was an ugly duckling.

The beauty that Eleanor developed was of a spiritual kind, for physically she always remained a plain woman. Eleanor's brows, lips and teeth were always a little too prominent. But she had a fine complexion, lovely soft hair and beautiful, intelligent blue eyes.

Almost prophetically Eleanor had written in her journal when she was only 14: ". . . no matter how plain a woman may be, if truth and loyalty are stamped upon her face, all will be attracted to her." Soon Eleanor's life began to change.

When she was 15, Eleanor's unhappy life under her

grandmother's control took a turn for the better. At the urging of her aunt and uncle—Edith and Teddy Roosevelt—Eleanor was sent to a boarding school near London, England. There, at Allenswood, she came under the influence of the headmistress, a strong-willed Frenchwoman, Marie Souvestre. Mademoiselle Souvestre took Eleanor under her wing and served as a model for the young and impressionable girl.

Mademoiselle Souvestre awakened Eleanor's innate curiosity and introduced her to most of the intellectual and aesthetic pleasures that life can offer. During school vacations, the pair traveled together throughout Europe. They savored everything—the sights, the cultural offerings and the people. Eleanor learned to enjoy good food, fine wines, lively conversation and stimulating company. These were some of the happiest years of Eleanor's life.

After three years under Mademoiselle's tutelage, Eleanor returned to New York to resume her role in society. She had wanted to stay at Allenswood to complete a fourth year, but Grandmother Hall would not hear of it.

Eleanor was a slender, tall and graceful girl, though never a beauty. She looked forward to entering the adult world, but she secretly feared that she would be unpopular and that young men would find her unattractive.

Soon Eleanor found work to do. She taught dance and calisthenics at the Rivington Street Settlement House on Manhattan's Lower East Side. In the early years of the 20th century this part of New York was a colorful neighborhood crowded with immigrants recently arrived from Europe.

Eleanor at the time of her marriage to Franklin Roosevelt in 1905

Eleanor and Franklin

In those days a girl of Eleanor's standing needed to marry quickly or she might lose her prospects. Eleanor was neither self-confident nor considered beautiful. Nor did she have the same kind of sophistication that most other young woman of her class displayed.

16

Luckily, her distant cousin Franklin Delano Roosevelt was among her circle of friends. They had met when they were younger. But they got to know each other when Eleanor was invited to Hyde Park for Franklin's 21st birthday party. FDR was handsome and intense. Franklin and Eleanor found that they had much in common. In the summer of 1903 Franklin asked Eleanor to visit the family summer home at Campobello. The two people enjoyed each other's company, and in that same year they were secretly engaged.

When they were married on St. Patrick's Day in 1905, Franklin was 23 and Eleanor was 20. At the service in New York City, President Theodore Roosevelt gave his beloved niece away.

Franklin and Eleanor made an interesting match because there were so many contrasts in their personalities. Eleanor was naive, innocent and high-minded. FDR was ambitious, frivolous and largely self-centered. Perhaps because her own childhood had been so painful, Eleanor became an extremely thoughtful and caring adult. She was always deeply sensitive to the problems of others.

Eleanor found herself pregnant six times between 1906 and 1916. Their first child was Anna, born in 1906. She was followed next by James in 1907, Elliott in 1910, Franklin, Jr., in 1914 and John in 1916. Another child, also named Franklin, Jr., died almost immediately after his birth in 1909.

Sara Roosevelt made Eleanor give up her teaching job at the Rivington Street Settlement House after her first child was born. She feared that Eleanor might bring disease into the family from her contact with the people there.

During the early years of their marriage Franklin went to law school. Because the family lived in New York City, he studied at Columbia. In the spring of 1907, Roosevelt passed the bar exam and was able to practice law in New York State.

Franklin and Eleanor Roosevelt with their five children

Franklin Roosevelt as a New York State Senator in 1910

FDR Goes into Politics

Franklin Delano Roosevelt entered politics hoping to follow the example of his fifth cousin, Theodore. He was an enthusiastic admirer of his famous relative, even though FDR chose the rival Democratic party.

FDR's political career began when he was elected to the New York State Senate in 1910. Shortly after, during World War I, President Woodrow Wilson named Roosevelt assistant secretary of the navy. He served in this capacity from 1913 to 1920. Oddly enough, this was an office that Theodore Roosevelt had also held, less than 20 years before.

In 1920, FDR was the unsuccessful Democratic candidate for vice president. The next year, though, tragedy struck the young politician while the family was vacationing at Campobello.

One warm August day, Roosevelt and several of his children had spent the afternoon sailing. It had been a hot day, and when they were finished sailing they went to help battle a brush fire on a nearby island. Dirty and exhausted, they all went swimming in the icy water before running back to the house.

By supper FDR was aching and felt a chill. The next day the first symptoms of disease had set in. Franklin's left leg was numb, and soon his right one was as well. He was confined to bed with a high temperature. Within a few days a specialist had confirmed the diagnosis of poliomyelitis.

Polio is a serious disease that attacks the muscle fibers. It destroyed much of the muscle tissue in FDR's legs and left him crippled. For more than three years, Franklin shunned the public eye as he struggled to adjust to his illness. At first he hoped for complete recovery. But as time went on it was obvious that this was not going to be the case.

Roosevelt struggled to have a meaningful and successful life despite his ailment. Most of the time he was confined to a wheelchair. With great difficulty Roosevelt learned to walk with the aid of crutches.

In 1924 Roosevelt appeared before the public for the first time since his illness to give a speech. And it was not until the sweeping election victory of 1928 that FDR's return to public life was complete. In that year he won the bid to become governor of New York State.

Franklin Roosevelt with his wife and mother at the time of his inauguration as governor of New York State in 1929

The Family and Politics

Sara Delano Roosevelt dominated FDR's marriage and political life as she had dominated FDR's childhood. The elder Mrs. Roosevelt was a woman with a great sense of her own importance. Throughout their marriage the Roosevelts always lived with Sara. And Sara continued to run their lives until her death in 1941.

Three years after Eleanor and Franklin were married, Sara Roosevelt presented them with a unique Christmas gift. These were adjacent town houses in New York City—one for Sara and one for the young couple. Joining the two houses was a common door that was never shut. At one point, Eleanor was so annoyed with this link that she tried to block the opening with heavy furniture.

Eleanor's interest in politics was slow to develop. She once admitted that at the time she married Franklin she did not know the difference between state and national legislatures.

Sometime near the end of World War I, Eleanor accidentally opened some letters that had been addressed to Franklin. In the letters she found evidence that Franklin was involved romantically with Lucy Mercer Rutherfurd. Mrs. Rutherfurd had previously served as Eleanor's social secretary. Eleanor offered to divorce Franklin, but he refused. Sara Roosevelt was also anxious to avoid a scandal that could rock the family foundations and ruin her son's political career.

From that point on, the Roosevelts' marriage became stiff and formal. But they remained together until Franklin died. In its way, it was one of the most remarkable and successful political partnerships ever.

Sara Roosevelt often spoiled her grandchildren. She frequently formed alliances with them in an effort to get around Eleanor. As the eldest, Anna was used most often in these schemes. Both parents loved Anna, but she favored her father. And since there was always a gulf between Eleanor and Franklin, Anna's strongest bond was with her father.

When Eleanor was away from the White House, Anna often served as official hostess. Eleanor could never forgive Anna the fact that Anna liked Lucy Rutherfurd and saw her in her father's company. These facts only came out after FDR's death and put a strain on Anna and Eleanor's relationship for a long time.

The two children Roosevelt seemed closest to were Elliott and James. Perhaps it was because they were the oldest boys. Both sons adored him. When Roosevelt gave his speech in 1924 nominating Al Smith as the governor of New York, he needed to get to the podium. It was son John who skillfully helped him there, without the aid of a wheelchair. John made it seem as if FDR were doing the job on his own. It was FDR's first major public appearance since the 1921 polio attack.

Because Eleanor was such an active woman, she did not have much time to spend with her children, particularly after they were grown up. But she would always rush to them when they needed her.

All four sons served with distinction in World War II. This made both Eleanor and Franklin intensely proud of their boys. Elliott, John and Franklin, Jr., served in Europe, while Jimmy was stationed in the Pacific. People who didn't like the Roosevelts, however, noted that all four boys were officers!

Partially because of FDR's duties, and partially because of the strain between FDR and Eleanor, the children grew up in chaos. Roosevelt loved to romp and roughhouse with his children. But he left disciplining them to Eleanor. This is perhaps one of the reasons why all the children developed difficult relationships with their mother.

All five eventually married—and divorced—at least once. Many people disapproved of the children—they were not precisely what the public expected of presidents' children. In later years, the five would often fight and argue among themselves. Eleanor loved them all individually, but there came a time when she almost never saw them together.

In 1927 Eleanor began teaching drama, literature and history at the Todhunter School in New York City. She kept up her teaching schedule even after FDR became the governor of New York State. Eleanor and her friends, Nancy Cook and Marion Dickerman, owned and ran the school. Eleanor hoped to put into practice the progressive ideas she had learned from her own mentor, Marie Souvestre.

Eleanor never felt entirely at home at Springwood. When Sara died in 1941, caretakers on the estate said that on the day of her death a gigantic tree fell down, even though there were no strong winds. And park rangers at Springwood report that Sara Roosevelt's ghost still haunts the home. Sightings of the ghost are often seen in or near Sara's room. In the mid 1980s a fire raged through the house, causing considerable damage. The fire started in Sara Roosevelt's sitting room.

Eleanor's unhappiness in the large house was one of the reasons FDR permitted her to build a small getaway house and camp for herself only a few miles away from Springwood. The little estate was called Val-Kill. It became Eleanor's refuge for years, and after her husband's death she lived there permanently.

On the Political Road

Eleanor learned about FDR's decision to run for governor of New York State from a radio broadcast. Events like this shattered the intimacy between the two. They remained cordial but distant. Without Eleanor's help FDR could not have managed the active political career he pursued. And after the polio attack in 1921 that left him paralyzed below the waist he became even more dependent on Eleanor's help and guidance.

In 1928 Roosevelt was elected governor of New York State. The term was for two years. He took the oath of office in Albany on January 1, 1929. Two years later he was reelected to the job.

In Albany, Eleanor Roosevelt became the governor's gracious first lady. She did her duties but also kept up a certain measure of independence. She continued to teach at Todhunter School in New York City. She shuttled back and forth several days a week between Albany, Hyde Park and Manhattan. Eleanor Roosevelt was laying the foundation for the kind of active life she would pursue when she got to the White House.

After her son was elected governor of New York, Sara Roosevelt began a major renovation of the Hyde Park home. She added another story to the house as well as large wings, including a new drawing room that doubled the family's living space. She thought that a governor should have a large and impressive home.

The home of the Franklin Roosevelts on East 65th Street in New York City

25

In the meantime, on October 24, 1929, the stock market crashed. The country began the downward economic spiral that would end in the Great Depression. The Republican president, Herbert Hoover, was swamped by the events and could do nothing to get the country out of its troubles.

This meant that the 1932 presidential election was wide open, particularly for a Democratic candidate. Such an opportunity could not be passed up by Franklin Roosevelt.

And so Roosevelt campaigned across the country. Many people felt his polio would slow him down. Also, because of the illness they thought he wouldn't have the strength to do the job of president. But FDR waged one of the most active presidential campaigns in history. He sped across the country, making campaign appearances and greeting crowds from a specially built platform at the rear of a special train. The November election was a triumph for Roosevelt: He carried 42 of the 48 states and received a huge popular majority of votes.

Governor Roosevelt shaking hands during his 1932 campaign for President

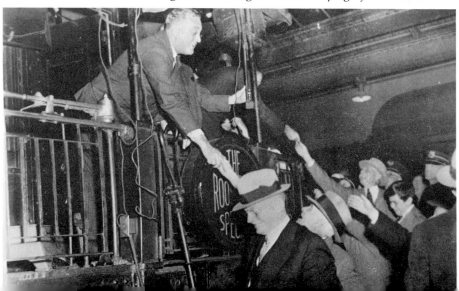

The Great Depression

Roosevelt's first two terms were largely concerned with restoring the nation's economy and helping the poor. The United States was in the middle of the Great Depression when Roosevelt came to office. He won the election by promising relief to victims of the ravaged economy. In his inaugural speech, Roosevelt reassured the American people with his words ". . . the only thing we have to fear is fear itself."

The stock market crash of 1929 was followed by widespread personal bankruptcies, business failures and bank closings. The depression touched just about everyone in the country. Millions were out of work or were forced into working only part-time. Other millions, not yet faced with want, feared they soon would be. It was in this atmosphere that FDR entered the White House.

The New Deal

Even after FDR took office, economic conditions in the country continued to worsen. By March of 1933 more than 13 million workers were unemployed. Almost every bank in the nation had failed.

Roosevelt had never known privation himself, yet many regarded him as a friend of the poor. Institutions such as unemployment insurance and programs like Social Security were FDR's creations.

Roosevelt was a visionary who dreamed of a "New Deal" for Americans and a new world order to ensure global peace. His domestic policy was designed to instill an unprecedented sense of security—and this was during the worst of the depression.

FDR worked to lift the United States out of its troubles with a sweeping program of reforms. These reforms were successful and did help to lessen unemployment.

Under Roosevelt's administration hundreds of new government agencies sprang into being. They offered immediate employment for thousands of out-of-work people. They were the first step in ending the Great Depression.

Many of the federal agencies created by Roosevelt exist today, including the Securities and Exchange Commission, the National Labor Relations Board, the Federal Communications Commission and the Federal Deposit Insurance Corporation. Roosevelt abolished child labor, brought electricity to rural America and built parks. He also promoted conservation with a host of unemployed young men whom he called the Civilian Conservation Corps.

President Roosevelt signing the Social Security Bill in 1935

Legislation was passed that would really help the common people: unemployment insurance, guaranteed minimum wages and insurance against poverty caused by an inability to work because of sickness or other misfortune. Other labor laws gave stricter controls over working conditions and hours.

Franklin Delano Roosevelt being sworn in as President of the United States in 1933

A Second Term

By 1936 there were some signs that the depression was lifting. Unemployment figures were dropping. American factories were beginning once more to turn out a steady stream of goods. Banks and other businesses were picking up. Most of the country felt that much of the economic recovery was due to Roosevelt's actions.

President Franklin D. Roosevelt (seated left), *Prime Minister Churchill* (seated beside him) *and members of the military, naval and diplomatic staffs, during religious services held at sea in August, 1941*

Roosevelt rode the wave of popularity through the 1936 presidential election to another landslide victory. This was probably the high point of his life and career. The mood was upbeat. It would be three more years until Europe was plunged into World War II. At 54 Roosevelt was still a vigorous man. The strains of piloting the country through the war years had not yet taken their toll.

On a global level, Roosevelt worked against the traditional U.S. policy of isolationism. He sought to position the United States as a leader working systematically with other nations to abolish war and establish world harmony.

American involvement in World War II was largely orchestrated through FDR's efforts. In 1941 it was inevitable that the United States would be drawn into the world conflict that had already involved so much of Europe. And now Asia, Australia and portions of Africa and South America were being called into action.

Critics of FDR say that the president and Congress helped engineer the disaster at Pearl Harbor on December 7, 1941. Intelligence reports had advance knowledge that the attack was coming. The base might have been better prepared for attack if the people there had been warned. This "surprise" bombing attack by the Japanese led directly to the American declaration of war on December 8.

A New Kind of First Lady

Following the inauguration in 1933 the Roosevelts moved into the White House. At first Eleanor feared that her role as first lady would isolate her from people and keep her from doing any real good. But she instantly took to her role. She was a tireless hostess. She was charming and friendly to everyone.

First Lady Eleanor Roosevelt as a sponsor for the Bear Mountain Camp for Unemployed Girls

For several years Mrs. Roosevelt wrote a daily newspaper column called "My Day." The column was printed in newspapers throughout the country. In it she candidly expressed her opinions on various political and social issues. In 1939 she learned just how powerful her position as first lady could be.

In February of that year Eleanor Roosevelt got into the middle of a great controversy. Washington, D.C., was considered a southern city, and in those years most public places in the South were segregated. The black American singer Marian Anderson was about to present a concert in Washington. The site chosen was Constitution Hall, a huge auditorium that would hold the enormous crowd expected for the event. The only problem was that the Daughters of the American Revolution (DAR) owned the hall and refused to allow the black singer to appear there.

The situation might not have been so bad except for one thing: Eleanor Roosevelt was a member of the DAR. When she found out about its racist stand, she was embarrassed and furious. She used her newspaper column to write a scathing indictment of the group. She publicly announced that she could no longer support the organization and resigned.

Another place for the concert still had to be found. On April 9, 1939 (Easter Sunday), a more fitting spot was chosen. Crowds surrounded the Lincoln Memorial. They filled all the possible places near the entrance to the memorial and spilled out over the lawn as far as anyone could see. Before a crowd estimated at more than 75,000 Marian

Eleanor Roosevelt cutting a ribbon to mark the formal opening of a New York City housing project

Anderson sang a program that ended with the Negro spiritual "Nobody Knows the Trouble I Seen."

Eleanor Roosevelt was not present. She felt that she had done what she needed to do. For her to attend would only have shifted the focus of the occasion away from Miss Anderson's performance.

Mrs. Roosevelt also broke with tradition by becoming a public figure in her own right. She held press conferences. She gave lectures and made radio broadcasts. She traveled to all parts of the United States and visited troops in the South Pacific during World War II. But these efforts also earned Mrs. Roosevelt many enemies. Some people resented her energy, her goodness and her unceasing work on behalf of worthy causes.

Eleanor Roosevelt was one of the first Americans to rely heavily on air travel. At a time when most people still preferred using the railroad and ships, Eleanor Roosevelt fearlessly logged thousands of air miles while she tackled new projects.

What many people did not understand was that Eleanor Roosevelt often served as her husband's "legs." Because his movements were severely limited, Mrs. Roosevelt frequently made many trips on his behalf. She was his "eyes" and "ears" as well. Eleanor recognized that her duties as first lady took precedence over her personal wishes. But it was a role that she accepted and welcomed. Eleanor transformed the position of first lady from that of simply being a hostess to one of political influence and activism.

In the White House

On Sunday, March 12, 1933, Roosevelt began what would come to be known as his "fireside chats." He had just become president and he wanted very much to keep in touch with the American people. These were radio broadcasts (there was no TV at that time) transmitted from the White House across the country to millions of Americans. Roosevelt had a pleasant voice and liked talking into the microphone and sharing experiences with his fellow Americans.

Roosevelt enjoyed talking to the public, and the people who heard these broadcasts were delighted at the simple and homey style of Roosevelt's talks. The fireside chats were a way of unifying Americans and helping them through

President Roosevelt during a "fireside chat"

the difficult times of the depression. Oddly enough, although the talks were labeled "fireside," the room from which they were broadcast did not have a working fireplace!

Christmas was one of the best times for the Roosevelts when they were living in the White House. Lilian Rogers Park was a maid in the White House for over 30 years. She wrote of Eleanor Roosevelt: "Christmastime was the best time to be at the White House. I have never seen a person more excited by the holiday season than Mrs. Roosevelt." On many Christmas Eves, FDR read Charles Dickens's *A Christmas Carol* to the gathered family after dinner.

Mrs. Roosevelt loved Christmas and delighted in shopping for gifts for family and friends. During her White House years she personally chose gifts for more than 200 people each Christmas. These she gave to her staff members and their families. She enjoyed finding just the right present for each person on her list.

In the summer of 1939 the Roosevelts hosted a visit to the White House by the reigning English monarchs, King George VI and Queen Elizabeth. Roosevelt and the king led a lengthy procession from the train station to the White House in an open car. Eleanor Roosevelt and the queen followed in a second car. It was a major visit and was typical of the kind of entertaining the Roosevelts did while they were in the White House.

On the same visit, the king and queen also spent time with the Roosevelts at their Hyde Park estate. The royal family was treated to a cookout and tasted American hot dogs, probably their first. On one leg of the visit, the singer Kate Smith was introduced quite simply to the royal couple by FDR: "This is Kate Smith. This is America."

President Roosevelt and King George VI of England in a Washington parade

Because of his polio, Roosevelt found it difficult to stand. His legs were supported by braces that weighed ten pounds each, and he really needed physical support from other people to stand for more than a brief time. But he did not want people to be aware of his handicap. So cameramen promised never to photograph him in his wheelchair. And there were many Americans who didn't realize how severely limited FDR was in his movements.

During Roosevelt's time in office, an indoor swimming pool was built at the White House. Swimming was considered good exercise for his damaged legs. The pool lasted until 1969 when President Nixon had it converted into a lobby for members of the press.

The five Roosevelt children were grown up by the time their parents moved into the White House. But many of the children—and their children's children—were frequent visitors there. And so were many aides and their families. It was an informal time for visitors, and they thronged to the great house in Washington.

After the attack on Pearl Harbor, everything changed. Much of the fun ended at the White House. It was important to maintain tight security during wartime and so the mansion was closed to the public. Secret bomb shelters were built underground, in the event of an airplane attack. And air raid wardens patrolled the grounds watching for the possible arrival of enemy planes.

Some of the social visits trailed off. But the distinguished visitors still came, including Madame Chiang Kai-shek of China, Winston Churchill of Great Britain and Soviet Minister Molotov.

Just before the war a huge program of renovation and reconstruction had been planned at the White House. But because of the war effort this, too, had to be put off. FDR's successor, Harry Truman, found much of the White House in such bad shape that he and his family had to move out shortly after they moved in.

The Roosevelt clan and their steady procession of guests had given the White House a hard workout. The wear and tear on the carpets and furnishings was great and was certainly a factor in the decision to renovate the mansion completely during the Truman administration. It took over five years for those renovations to be made.

It was during the war that a woodland retreat for the president was first established about 60 miles away from Washington in the Catoctin Hills of nearby Maryland. Roosevelt called it Shangri-la, but it was later renamed Camp David.

Eleanor Roosevelt hardly ever went there. Nothing could disguise the fact that the Roosevelts themselves sometimes didn't see much of each other. Dinner was often the only part of the day when they were together. They both kept busy and independent schedules.

Eleanor made the White House as cozy as possible and brought much of their furniture from their Hyde Park home. She also made sure that the furnishings at the White House were placed so it would be easy for the president to get around. FDR had a well-known dog, a Scottie named Fala, who went with the Roosevelts across the United States and throughout the world. And Roosevelt had a car specially equipped with hand gears so that he could drive anywhere he wanted with some independence.

Eleanor and Franklin Roosevelt with their 13 grandchildren. This is the last family photo taken before the president's death.

The Longest Presidency

In 1940 Roosevelt was easily reelected president for a third term. The war had begun in Europe and the economy had stabilized. It seemed comfortable for FDR to be in office. It was the first—and last—time that a president served more than two terms. In 1951 the 22nd Amendment to the Constitution was passed. This amendment put a limit on the number of times a person can be elected president: only twice.

The 1944 election was also an easy one for Roosevelt to win. Victory in World War II was in sight and it seemed natural for FDR to remain until the war was actually over. But a few people noticed that Roosevelt looked frail and unwell.

In 1945, because of Roosevelt's failing health, his fourth inauguration was held at the White House. Only once before had the ceremony been held at the executive mansion.

By that time the Roosevelts had 13 grandchildren. There is a photograph of Eleanor and Franklin, looking old and drawn, with these grandchildren. It was the last family photo taken. Less than three months later Roosevelt was dead.

The funeral procession of Franklin Delano Roosevelt

FDR was president longer than any other president and lived in the White House longer than any other. Along with Churchill, de Gaulle and Stalin, he became one of the great leaders of the World War II period. He died only a few weeks before the war ended in Europe. He knew that peace was on the horizon, but he did not live long enough to see it come.

As the war was winding down, FDR's health began to fail. In April of 1945 he was vacationing in Warm Springs, Georgia. With him was his old friend Lucy Mercer Rutherfurd. On April 12 FDR was sitting for a portrait when he was stricken with a cerebral hemorrhage. He died just a few hours later without regaining consciousness. Although he looked much older, Roosevelt was only 63.

Roosevelt died just two months into his fourth term, leaving his successor, Vice President Harry Truman, to complete the work that Roosevelt had begun. Many people felt that Vice President Truman was not suited for the task. In fact, when Truman first saw Eleanor Roosevelt after her husband's death and he inquired, "What can we do for you?" her response was, "Oh, no, what can we do for *you*?"

Roosevelt's body was taken on a long journey by train from Georgia to Hyde Park, New York. The procession stopped long enough for a state funeral service in Washington, D.C. There, a wagon, or caisson, carried Roosevelt's body through the crowded streets. That same caisson was used again on another sad occasion. In 1963 it formed part of the procession that carried John F. Kennedy's body through many of the same Washington streets during his funeral ceremonies.

After leaving Washington, the train carrying Roosevelt's body moved slowly up the East Coast. It finally reached Roosevelt's Hyde Park home. There, in the rose garden at his beloved Springwood estate, he was buried.

Mrs. Eleanor Roosevelt boarding a plane to attend a meeting of the Human Rights Commission of the United States at Geneva, Switzerland

First Lady of the World

Roosevelt had had great plans for the postwar world. One of these was the dream of the United Nations, a group that would forever hold nations together and keep wars from breaking out. As it happened, he did not live to see his dream become a reality. But his wife was on hand to introduce and carry out many of Roosevelt's proposals.

Eleanor Roosevelt's long career in public life did not end with her husband's death. She continued to devote her energies to the victims of prejudice, poverty and war. She stayed in the Hyde Park area, living simply in her hideaway home, Val-Kill, near the larger Roosevelt family estate.

In 1946 Eleanor Roosevelt was appointed American spokesperson to the newly formed United Nations. She was chairperson of the commission that drafted the U.N.'s Universal Declaration of Human Rights. It was during this time that Mrs. Roosevelt was given the title "First Lady of the World."

Eleanor Roosevelt along with former New York Governor and Senator, Herbert H. Lehman (left), *honoring the Reverend Dr. Martin Luther King, Jr., in 1961*

Mrs. Roosevelt remained active in social and political life until 1962, when her health began to decline. In November of that year she died in New York City. Many prominent leaders, including then President John F. Kennedy, attended her funeral. She was buried at Hyde Park next to her husband. A simple stone marker stands on top of the resting place of two of the most significant figures of the 20th century.

For Further Reading

Anthony, Carl Sferrazza. *First Ladies: The Saga of the Presidents' Wives and Their Power, 1789–1961*. New York: William Morrow and Company, Inc., 1990.

Devaney, John. *Franklin Delano Roosevelt, President*. New York: Walker and Company, 1987.

Fisher, Leonard Everett. *The White House*. New York: Holiday House, 1989.

Freedman, Russell. *Franklin Delano Roosevelt*. New York: Clarion Books, 1990.

Friedel, Frank. *The Presidents of the United States of America*. Revised edition. Washington, D.C.: The White House Historical Association, 1989.

Greenblatt, Miriam. *Franklin Delano Roosevelt*. Ada, Okla.: Garrett Educational Corporation, 1989.

Israel, Fred L. *Franklin Delano Roosevelt*. New York: Chelsea House Publishers, 1985.

Klapthor, Margaret Brown. *The First Ladies*. Revised edition. Washington, D.C.: The White House Historical Association, 1989.

Lindsay, Rae. *The Presidents' First Ladies*. New York: Franklin Watts, 1989.

The Living White House. Revised edition. Washington, D.C.: The White House Historical Association, 1987.

St. George, Judith. *The White House: Cornerstone of a Nation*. New York: G. P. Putnam's Sons, 1990.

Scharf, Lois. *Eleanor Roosevelt, First Lady of American Liberalism*. Boston: Twayne Publishers, 1987.

Taylor, Tim. *The Book of Presidents*. New York: Arno Press, 1972.

Toor, Rachel. *Eleanor Roosevelt*. New York: Chelsea House Publishers, 1989.

The White House. Washington, D.C.: The White House Historical Association, 1987.

Index